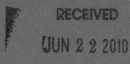

# How does a BONE become a FOSSIL?

Melissa Stewart

Chicago, Illinois

## www.heinemannraintree.com
Visit our website to find out more information about Heinemann-Raintree books.

## To order:
☎ Phone 888-454-2279
💻 Visit www.heinemannraintree.com to browse our catalog and order online.

©2010 Raintree
an imprint of Capstone Global Library, LLC
Chicago, Illinois

Edited by David Andrews and Laura Knowles
Designed by Richard Parker and Wagtail
Original illustrations © Capstone Global Library, LLC 2010
Illustrated by Jeff Edwards
Picture research by Hannah Taylor and Sally Claxton
Originated by Modern Age Repro House Ltd
Printed and Bound in the United States by Corporate Graphics

14 13 12 11 10
10 9 8 7 6 5 4 3 2 1

**Library of Congress Cataloging-in-Publication Data**
Stewart, Melissa.
   How does a bone become a fossil? / Melissa Stewart.
      p. cm. -- (How does it happen?)
   Includes bibliographical references and index.
   ISBN 978-1-4109-3445-1 (hc) -- ISBN 978-1-4109-3453-6 (pb)
   1. Fossilization--Juvenile literature. 2. Fossils--Juvenile literature. I. Title.
   QE721.2.F6S74 2008
   560--dc22
                        2008052596

**Acknowledgments**
The author and publishers are grateful to the following for permission to reproduce copyright material: Alamy pp. **5** (© Wolfgang Kaehler), **6** (© blickwinkel), **7** (© Robert Harding Picture Library Ltd.), **14** (© Jupiter Images/Thinkstock), **15** (© Robert Harding Picture Library Ltd), **19** (© Danita Delimont), **22** (© Wendy Temple), **24** (© Nature Picture Library), **26** (© The Natural History Museum), **28** (© Tim Cuff); Corbis pp. **20** (Louie Psihoyos), **27** (Reuters/Carlos Barria), **29** (Jonathan Blair); istockphoto **background image** (© Dean Turner); Science Photo Library pp. **4** (CHRISTIAN JEGOU PUBLIPHOTO DIFFUSION), **12** (Mark Garlick), **13** (STEVE TAYLOR), **16** (JIM AMOS), **17** (DAVID R. FRAZIER), **18** (SINCLAIR STAMMERS), **21** (CHRISTIAN DARKIN), **23** (Ria Novosti), **25** (PASIEKA).

Cover photographs of a gray triggerfish (*Balistes Capriscus*) skeleton found along the Pacific coast in Baja California, Mexico (top) reproduced with permission of Photolibrary/Phototake Science/Scott Camazine and a fish fossil in rock (bottom) reproduced with permission of Alamy/©David R. Frazier Photolibrary, Inc.

Every effort has been made to contact copyright holders of any material reproduced in this book. Any omissions will be rectified in subsequent printings if notice is given to the publisher.

# Contents

Some words are shown in bold, **like this**. You can find out what they mean by looking in the glossary.

# Signs of Past Life

Long ago, our world was a very different place. Life was only present in the oceans and no animals or plants lived on land.

*Eusthenopteron* was a genus (group of similar types) of fish that swam in the sea about 385 million years ago. Its name means "strong fin."

This painting shows a variety of animals that lived in Earth's oceans 300 to 700 million years ago.

## Back-up breathing

*Eusthenopteron* had a big advantage over other fish. It could breathe in two different ways. Most of the time, it took in the gas oxygen through its gills. But it also had sacs that worked like lungs to get extra oxygen from the air. Animals need oxygen to live and grow.

The last *Eusthenopteron* died millions of years ago. This kind of fish disappeared long before the first humans lived. It became **extinct** long before the age of dinosaurs, too.

If you want to know what *Eusthenopteron* looked like, you can go to a museum. But do not expect to see bodies with fins and scales. After millions of years, the bodies are long gone. All that remains are **fossils**, or pieces of evidence of this ancient life.

*Eusthenopteron foordi*

*Eusthenopteron* fossil

*Eusthenopteron* lived in oceans all over the world. This fossil was found in Miguasha National Park in Quebec, Canada.

# Two Kinds of Fossil

Scientists study **fossils** to find out how creatures lived long ago. They also find out how life on Earth has changed over time.

**Body fossils** are the remains of plants, animals, and other creatures that were once alive. Dinosaur bones, shark teeth, and seashells are all body fossils. So are **petrified** trees (trees that have turned to stone) and leaf **imprints**. These fossils show us what life was like millions of years ago.

Fossilized shark teeth show us that sharks have lived in Earth's oceans for millions of years.

*Shark teeth*

Dinosaur footprints

A scientist examines part of the world's longest dinosaur trackway. It is located in Bolivia, a country in South America.

**Trace fossils** tell us something about how ancient creatures lived. Dinosaur footprints, **coprolites** (animal droppings), and vomit are all trace fossils. So are tooth marks and stomach stones, unhatched eggs, and ancient animal homes. These fossils help us understand how ancient creatures moved, what they ate, and how they raised their young.

Many scientists study body fossils and trace fossils together. That gives them the clearest picture of the ancient world.

**7**

# From Fish to Fossil

Dead *Eusthenopteron* sank to the muddy seafloor. Although soft body parts rotted away, hard bones were left behind.

A fish's bones have a lot in common with our bones. They help a fish move and also protect its soft body parts.

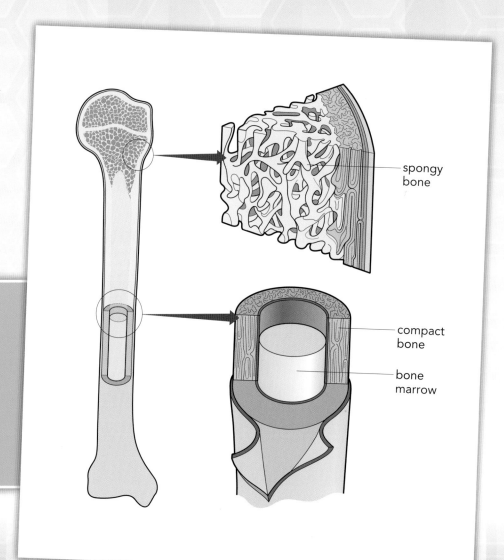

spongy bone

compact bone

bone marrow

Many animals' bones have a hard outer layer and are softer on the inside.

Most bones have two layers. Hard **compact bone** is on the outside. It is made up of rings of **minerals** (natural solid materials). The softer inside layer is called **spongy bone**. It is full of tiny holes that contain bone marrow, a kind of tissue. New blood cells are made in the bone marrow.

Like bone, water contains lots of minerals. When bones are surrounded by water for a long time, minerals in the water replace the original bone.

Over millions of years, minerals from ocean water took the place of the minerals in *Eusthenopteron* bones. Then they hardened to form **fossils**. The hard stone looked just like *Eusthenopteron* bones.

## Magical fossils?

In the past, people did not understand how fossils form. Some people thought fossils were magical rocks that could keep milk fresh, bring good luck, or ward off evil spirits.

# Buried Treasure

While *Eusthenopteron* **skeletons** were turning into **fossils**, layers of mud and sand piled up on top of the bones. The weight of the top layers pushed down on the lower layers.

Over millions of years, this fish's skeleton becomes a fossil. If the fossil is exposed, people can dig it up and study it.

Over time, the mud and sand stuck together. Then they hardened to form rock. The fish fossils were trapped deep underground.

As more time passed, the land around the fossils changed. An earthquake may have shifted the land and brought some fossils to the surface.

Wind or water could have slowly eroded (worn away) the rock above other fossils. After millions of years, parts of fish fossils stuck out of the ground.

People noticed *Eusthenopteron* fossils and dug them up. Then scientists studied the fossils to find out when *Eusthenopteron* lived and how it survived.

## What's in a name?

Scientists who study fossils are called **paleontologists**. The word *paleontologist* comes from a Greek word that means "those who study ancient things." The word *fossil* comes from a Latin word that means "dug up."

# Where Fossils Form

*Tyrannosaurus rex* is one of the largest meat-eating dinosaurs scientists have found.

Modern humans have lived on Earth for about 200,000 years. But dinosaurs ruled the land for 165 million years.

How many dinosaurs lived during all that time? Billions of them existed, but most of them did not leave behind **fossils**. Many dead dinosaur bodies, including the bones, were eaten. Others rotted away.

For a fossil to form, the conditions had to be just right. The body of a dead creature had to be covered with mud or sand soon after it died. The built-up layers of mud, sand, and other materials—called sediment— protected the **skeleton** from the sun, wind, and rain.

Most fossils are found in rock that was once underwater. That is why the most common fossils are the remains of ocean creatures.

Petrified logs, Arizona

These petrified logs were once part of a giant forest that grew in Arizona.

## Fossil forests

Bone is not the only material that can turn to stone. **Petrified** Forest National Park in Arizona contains thousands of logs that became fossils after their wood was replaced by **minerals**. Scientists think the huge trees died about 225 million years ago.

# Common Body Fossils

Scientists have discovered many **fossils** of fish bones. But shark teeth are the easiest **body fossils** to find. Why? Because there are so many of them.

A shark's teeth grow in rows. When a tooth falls out, the one behind it moves to fill the space.

Sharks have lived on Earth for 450 million years. They are constantly losing old teeth and growing new ones. A shark may lose up to 10,000 teeth in its lifetime. That is a lot of teeth!

**Ammonites** first lived in Earth's oceans around 240 million years ago. Like lobsters and snails, ammonites were **invertebrates** (animals without a **spine** or other bones). Their soft bodies were surrounded by hard, spiral-shaped shells. Today, ammonites are long gone. But people often find fossils of their hard shells.

These ammonite fossils formed as layers of limestone built up around them. Limestone is made of the crushed shells of tiny ocean creatures.

*Ammonite fossils*

More than 10,000 kinds of **trilobites** lived in the ocean 540 million years ago. The last of these invertebrates died about 250 million years ago. But people find fossils of their hard outer coverings in rocks all over the world.

Scientists have also found many ancient fossils of sea stars, sea urchins, clams, and scallops.

# Dinosaur Fossils

When someone says the word *fossil*, you probably think of dinosaurs. Maybe you have even seen models of *Tyrannosaurus*, *Triceratops*, *Seismosaurus*, and other giant beasts at a museum. But did you know that scientists have discovered fossils from fewer than 3,000 dinosaurs in the whole world?

Most of the dinosaur fossils **paleontologists** have dug up come from small animals. But some are bigger than a bus. Imagine what it would be like to discover one of them.

A scientist works carefully to unearth a dinosaur at Dinosaur National Monument in Utah.

That is what happened to a U.S. fossil hunter named Susan Hendrickson. In 1990 she spotted some bits of bone fossils in a cliff in South Dakota. They were part of the largest and most complete *Tyrannosaurus rex* ever found. Today, the dinosaur, named Sue, is on display at the Field Museum of Natural History in Chicago, Illinois.

'Sue' the Tyrannosaurus rex

Can you imagine how excited Susan Hendrickson must have been when she discovered this giant dinosaur?

## Did you know?

*Seismosaurus* is the longest dinosaur ever found. It could grow as long as four school buses parked end to end. The giant plant eater lived in the western part of North America about 145 million years ago.

# Molds and Casts

Even when an animal's bones or other hard body parts break down, a **fossil** may still form. If layers of mud harden around a dinosaur's bone or a **trilobite's** outer covering before it disappears, an **imprint** is left behind in the rock. This kind of fossil is called a **mold**. If the mold fills with **minerals** that harden to stone, a **cast** will form.

Trilobite fossil

This cast formed from the body of a trilobite that once lived in what is now Wales, a country in Great Britain.

Once in a while, soft body parts, like the skin of a dinosaur or the leaf from a tree, leave behind imprints. They form when the skin or leaf presses deep into the soft seafloor or the muddy ground in a swamp. As the ground hardens, the marks harden, too.

Antarctica

Ferns once grew on this land in Antarctica.

## Frozen ferns

Some ferns can grow only in hot, sunny places. But scientists have found imprints of these ferns in Antarctica—the coldest continent on Earth. How could this happen? Believe it or not, the land on Earth has moved over time. Millions of years ago, Antarctica was warmer because it was closer to the equator, an imaginary line around the middle of Earth.

# Traces of the Past

What can scientists learn from **trace fossils**? They can learn all kinds of things.

- **Coprolites** and vomit tell us where and when animals lived and what they ate.

## Dino droppings

In 1995 a Canadian **fossil** hunter named Wendy Sloboda found a huge coprolite in Canada. It was the size of two loaves of bread placed end to end. Scientists think it may have been left behind by a *Tyrannosaurus rex*.

This scientist is studying a large collection of coprolites.

*Coprolites*

- Ancient dinosaur nests show us how many eggs the dinosaurs laid at one time and how much care the parents gave their young.

- A trail of dinosaur footprints helps us understand how an animal moved, how tall it was, and how much it weighed.

This computer artwork of a dinosaur protecting its nest from a predator could not have been made without the information learned from trace fossils.

*Protoceratops guarding its eggs*

- Giant stone termite mounds in Gallup, New Mexico, help us understand how the ancient insects lived.

- Tooth marks provide clues about how prehistoric predators (animals that kill other animals) hunted, and what they ate.

- Stomach stones show us where plant-eating dinosaurs lived and how they digested their food.

21

# Trapped in Tar and Ice

About 65 million years ago, all the dinosaurs on Earth became **extinct**. That meant **mammals** could take over all the places where dinosaurs had lived. (A mammal is an animal that has a **spine** and feeds its young with mother's milk.) Over time, mammals grew larger and larger. They spread out all over the world.

Just like dinosaurs, mammals left behind **fossils**. Scientists have discovered some mammal fossils in rock. Others have been found in some very strange places.

These model mammoths show how animals became trapped in tar long ago.

Rancho La Brea Tar Pits, Los Angeles

In the early 1900s, people started to pull fossils of woolly mammoths, saber-toothed cats, giant ground sloths, and early horses out of the Rancho La Brea Tar Pits in Los Angeles, California. All these animals had lived about 40,000 years ago. They died when they were trapped in large, shallow puddles of thick, sticky tar.

*Discovery of a baby mammoth*

In 1989, workers pulled this baby mammoth out of the icy ground in northern Russia.

Scientists working in Russia have found several woolly mammoths trapped in ice. Some of the fossils still have skin, hair, and soft inner organs. Scientists think these mammoths died when mudflows quickly buried the animals. Over time, layers of ice built up around the bodies and froze them.

# What Is Amber?

Some ancient trees oozed a thick, sticky liquid called **resin**. Over millions of years, the resin dried and hardened to form **amber**.

Some modern trees ooze resin, too. This sticky, golden liquid is dripping off an almond tree.

Oozing resin

Amber is a beautiful yellowish-brown material that some people use to make jewelry. Sometimes amber contains bits of plants or tiny creatures that got stuck in the resin.

Scientists have found chunks of amber with flies, ants, mosquitoes, spiders, and small worms inside. They have even discovered pieces of amber that contain small frogs and lizards.

In 2001 a U.S. scientist named Lynn Margulis accidentally dropped a piece of amber with a 20-million-year-old termite inside. Since the amber was broken, she decided to drill into tiny bubbles near the

A mosquito in amber

This tiny midge got itself into a sticky situation about 40 million years ago. Today, it is preserved in amber.

termite's body and see what was inside. She found ancient gas produced by bacteria—tiny, one-celled creatures—living in the termite's gut.

## The oldest feathers

Scientists know that the first birds lived about 150 million years ago. But until 2000, the only sign of their feathers were **imprints**. That is when scientists working in France found seven feathers stuck inside a 100-million-year-old piece of amber. They are the oldest feathers on Earth.

# Scientists at Work

This scientist is using small tools to carefully chip away at the rock surrounding a fossil.

To find **fossils**, scientists go to deserts and other places where plants do not cover the ground. They look for rocks that formed millions of years ago. Then they hunt for bits of bone and other signs of fossils in the rock.

When the scientists spot something, they take measurements and make drawings of the area. Then they start digging.

At first, workers use axes, shovels, and jackhammers to break open the rock. When they get close to the fossil, scientists use small tools to chip away tiny pieces of rock. They work slowly and carefully for hours, days, or even weeks.

Finally, the scientists cover the fossil in a pasty material called plaster and lift it out of the ground. The plaster dries and hardens to protect the fossil while it travels back to the laboratory. Then the scientists study the fossil closely.

This scientist is working on a fossil that has been protected with a layer of plaster.

## Did you know?

In the 1870s, scientists working in Colorado and Wyoming found many large dinosaur fossils. That is when people in the United States started to become interested in ancient life on Earth.

# Be a Fossil Hunter

**Fossils** are easier to find than you might think. No matter where you live, there are probably some fossils nearby. There might even be some in your neighborhood. The next time you see a rock, pick it up and look at it closely. Can you see a fossil inside?

A family hunt for fossils on a beach in Great Britain.

Fossil hunting

You probably will not find a dinosaur bone, but you might spot some shark teeth or small sea animals. Once you learn how to look for fossils, you can find them almost anywhere.

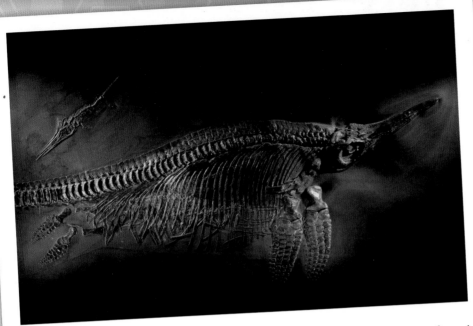

An Ichthyosaurus fossil

*Ichthyosaurus* fossils have been found in North and South America and Europe.

## Kids can do it!

Sometime around 1811, when Mary Anning was about 12 years old, she discovered the first *Ichthyosaurus* fossils near her home in Lyme Regis, England. *Ichthyosaurus* was a large reptile that lived in the ocean.

To get started, call local museums. Ask them to suggest some good places to look for fossils. They might even offer field trips for fossil hunters.

If you find a fossil, a field guide can help you identify it. If you think it is a really interesting fossil, contact a **paleontologist**. You never know what you might find.

# Glossary

**amber** dried, hardened resin (the sticky liquid some plants produce)

**ammonite** invertebrate with a spiral-shaped shell. Ammonites lived in the ocean around 240 million years ago.

**body fossil** remains of plants, animals, and other creatures that were once alive

**cast** fossil that forms when minerals harden inside a mold

**compact bone** hard outer surface of all bones. Some bones contain only compact bone.

**coprolite** fossilized animal dropping

**extinct** die out or disappear from Earth forever

**fossil** any evidence of ancient life

**imprint** shape sometimes left in built-up layers of mud, sand, and other materials before a bone rots

**invertebrate** animal with no spine or other bones

**mammal** animal that has a spine and feeds its young with mother's milk

**mineral** natural solid material

**mold** fossil of an imprint

**paleontologist** scientist who studies fossils

**petrified** turned to stone or another hard substance

**resin** thick, sticky liquid some plants produce for protection from insects

**skeleton** all the bones that make up an animal's body

**spine** bones that run down an animal's back and support it

**spongy bone** soft, flexible tissue inside some bones

**trace fossil** evidence of how an ancient creature lived

**trilobite** invertebrate with a hard outer covering. Trilobites were common in Earth's oceans for millions of years, but disappeared about 250 million years ago.

# Find Out More

## Books to read

Do you still have questions about bones and fossils? There is much more to learn about these fascinating topics. You can find out more by picking up some of these books from your local library:

Arnold, Caroline. *Global Warming and Dinosaurs: Fossil Discoveries at the Poles*. New York: Clarion, 2009.

Kudlinski, Kathleen V. *Boy, Were We Wrong About Dinosaurs!* New York: Puffin, 2008.

Sloan, Christopher. *Bizarre Dinosaurs: Some Very Strange Creatures and Why We Think They Got That Way*. Washington, D.C.: National Geographic, 2008.

## Websites to explore

If you're curious about dinosaur eggs, check out this site:
**www.nationalgeographic.com/features/96/dinoeggs**

Explore this site to discover how Earth has changed over time and what prehistoric life was like:
**www.fieldmuseum.org/evolvingplanet**

Think it would be fun to visit a petrified forest? Find out more about the one in Arizona:
**www.nps.gov/pefo**

Get the buzz on a recent dinosaur trackway discovery:
**www.smm.org/buzz/buzz_tags/fossil_footprints**

# Index